A SOUTH AFRICA

TIGER BOOKS INTERNATIONAL

Text
Alberto Salza

Graphic Design
Anna Galliani

Map
Arabella Lazzarin

Translation
Antony Shugaar

Contents

1 *In this photograph one has an excellent view of a stretch of coastline of the Cape of Good Hope, near Camps Bay.*

2-3 *The warm light of sunset envelops Clifton Bay, a very popular beach not far from Cape Town.*

4-5 *The valley of the river Hex, in the Cape province, is transformed in the fall: the leaves of the grape vines in fact become a brilliant red. Here the climate is Mediterranean in its mildness, behind the shelter of the mountains of Kwadousberg.*

6-7 *The arch of the Wolfberg, or Mountain of the Wolf, is one of the most remarkable rock formations that can be found in the Cedarberg chain.*

8 *This picture depicts a Zulu girl. The Zulus are one of the most important ethnic groups in South Africa, both in terms of numbers and in terms of social and political organization. This girl comes from the village of Ixopo, just a few miles to the south of Pietermaritzburg. The name of the village comes from a little swamp that the Zulus called exobo, from the sound that someone makes when trying to extricate their feet from the mud, the very same mud that is sometimes used by girls to decorate their faces.*

9 *In the Kalahari Gemsbok Park, at the northernmost point of South Africa, the sands are a bright reddish color. This is the edge of the Kalahari desert, the "Land of Thirst."*

12-13 *A herd of buffalo slakes its thirst in the river Sabie Sabie, to the southwest of the Kruger park. Along the river is a private reserve, one of the best places to observe wild animals of the savannah.*

14-15 *Despite the ongoing process of urbanization, it is still possible to find long stretches of unspoilt beaches along the southern coast of the Cape.*

16-17 *The rocky peninsula of the Cape of Good Hope, here seen from the southeast, divides the Atlantic Ocean from the Indian Ocean. The entire cape is about fifty miles in length, and was first rounded by a European in the year 1488. The European in question was the Portuguese navigator Bartolomé Diaz, who lost his ship in these same waters upon his return from the Indies two years later.*

18-19 *This photograph shows the waterfalls of the river Orange, inside the Augrabies National Park, in the northern area of the Cape province. Here one of the largest rivers in South Africa leaps downward three hundred feet through the crags from the plateau, reaching the flood plains that stretch out toward the Atlantic Ocean.*

This edition published in 1995 by TIGER BOOKS INTERNATIONAL PLC, 26a York Street Twickenham TW1 3LJ, England.

First published by Edizioni White Star. Title of the original edition: Sudafrica, un paradiso tra due oceani. © World copyright 1995 by Edizioni White Star, Via Candido Sassone 22/24, 13100 Vercelli, Italy.

ISBN 1-85501-688-5

Printed in Singapore by Tien Wah Press. Colour separation by La Cromografica, Ghemme (Novara) Italy.

BO

KALAHARI
DESERT

NAMIBIA

Orange River

KIM

N a m a q u a l a n d

ATLANTIC
OCEAN

REPUBLIC O
SOUTH AFR

CAPE PROVINCE

Nuweldbere

Lambert's Bay

Great
Karoo

CAPE TOWN ●

Little
Karoo

Cape of
Good Hope   False Bay

● Cape Agulhas

ZIMBABWE

MOZAMBIQUE

ANA

TRANSVAAL

KRUGER
NATIONAL
PARK

● PRETORIA

JOHANNESBURG ●

SWAZILAND

Vaal River

ORANGE
FREE STATE

Y ●

LESOTHO

NATAL

Drakensberge

● DURBAN

● EAST LONDON

● Port Elizabeth

NDIAN OCEAN

Introduction

I met Cecil John Rhodes once. In fact, it was he who first brought me to South Africa. I am, of course, talking about the grandson of the adventurer by the same name (businessman, we would call him today) who became the legend of South Africa: he began by planting cotton, and wound up with a harvest of gold and diamonds. "My" Rhodes, on the other hand, bred livestock and was, when I met him, over sixty years old. He loaded me like a bag of potatoes onto his unhinged two-seater airplane, which stood on a horrible airstrip in the Kalahari desert. The takeoff was really just a series of jounces and leaps, with a lurch into a pothole to avoid a goat and a hurtle over a fence post or two. I though to myself that Rhodes had spent his entire lifetime working to become the worst pilot south of the Equator. He flew in a remarkable manner, and never glanced at his instruments. "If you want to know where we are," he told me, "we can fly low and take a look at the signs on the farms." With God looking over us, we landed secretly in a god-forsaken place in South Africa, Rhodes performed his mysterious errands, I escaped arrest for our numerous crimes, and we left. South Africans are just that way.

Since then, my trips to South Africa have become more frequent, more legal, and I have learned to use the appropriate vehicles. I have heard nothing more about Rhodes, but South Africa seen from above has never left my mind's eye, as if in the interactive memory of a videogame with sophisticated graphics. The overall vision tells one that nature has simply outdone herself in South Africa. Geology and climate have carved out a great variety of landscapes. To the northwest appears the desert, slowly merging into the bush-covered Karoos. In the south, one leaves an antarctic ocean to reach harsh daunting coasts and a mild climate. To the east, the savannah runs along the edge of portions of tropical rain forest. To the southeast, the hills of Natal are gentle and the sea grows warm, between lagoons and barrier reefs. A little further inland, one can see the snow-covered summits of high mountains.

As people say down here, South Africa is "a world apart." This is an ancient subcontinent. If we focus carefully on the reliefs that one encounters just prior to reaching Lesotho, our interactive video game will bring us to a grassy plain from which enormous round boulders jut up. These are *kopje*, granite "heads" that seem like the bones of an immense creature buried beneath the savannah. They are four billion years old, and only

16

Greenland boasts boulders that are more venerable in age. The *kopje* are the remains of the South African craton, the first solid island in the great southern magma. In the valleys of the Barberton mountains, along the border with Swaziland, a microphotograph of the rocks will reveal traces of tiny organisms. These are algae and bacteria from three billion years previous: these are the first forms of life to appear on earth. South Africa is always on the hunt for primates. Around here, in Taung, Sterkfontein, Swartkrans, Makapansgat, and elsewhere, fossils of the earliest hominids are found in great abundance, the remains of our earliest ancestors. Beginning three million years ago, a few bipedal apes, still potential prey for prowling leopards, were trying out stone technology, developing abstract thought, increasing the size of their skulls, and attempting to develop speech. South Africa was the first behavioural laboratory for the human race. And it was from a cave along the Klasies river, a little stream that runs into the Indian Ocean just west of Port Elizabeth, that the first *Homo sapiens sapiens* set out to conquer the world, the first of our species, one hundred twenty thousand years ago. If one looks at central South Africa from the sky, the undertaking of Klasies man seems quite impossible. This is the Karoo, the "Land of the Great Thirst," as the Hottentots described it when the first white men arrived. The word "Hottentot" is a pejorative, and it derives from the Old Dutch term *stotter* (stutter) and referred to the clicking sounds of the language of the *khoi-khoi*, as the Hottentots refer to themselves.

The Karoo is a desolate plateau which, ever since I made my first flight, has attracted me with what might be called the "allure of horror." Imagine billions of tiny shrubs that survive on nothing: if you were to live there, you would have the distinct impression that it never rains there. And yet the entire region is inhabited by humans: the territory is divided up into farms of enormous size, where the main activity is breeding sheep. In order to survive, a single sheep might need as much as seven acres. And yet, a quarter of a billion years ago, this area was a valley covered with glaciers. Then Antarctica sailed away, following the continental drift. The climate changed and the Karoo became a partially salty marsh. The sun grew warmer, and the ground emerged from the mud. The Karoo became the domain of dinosaurs. In the arid dirt of the Karoo, it is possible to find fossils of a thousand different species. In the area around Fraserburg, a certain Mr. Visser, an extraordinary expert on the ecology of the Karoo, showed me extensive areas of sandstone in which reptiles, large and small, had left their tracks. Visser also showed me the minuscule florets that adorn the grim bushes of the Karoo. Then Visser pushed aside a clump of grass, and there appeared the entire skeleton of a mammalian reptile, a warm-blooded creature that, by the time the

dinosaurs became extinct, had already evolved into the first, tiny mammals. Were it not for the Karoo, we would never have made it onto the face of the earth.

An expanse of sand and flowers carries us on to Namaqualand, on the Atlantic coast. Here one feels the effects of the icy Antarctic currents. The cold prevents rain from falling in any abundance. The area is a semidesert that runs right down to the edge of the sea. If you happen to go there at the time of the first rains in late August, you will see a explosive regeneration of life unlike anything found elsewhere in the world. Here, the average rainfall is only 6.3 inches per year, and drought is a way of life. When, however, a little water does drizzle down, people smile at you and say, "It'll be a good year for flowers," as if their survival depended on the petals of the wild gladioli. At Lambert's Bay, there is an island teeming with penguins and otters, who swim amidst the ocean waves, while the thousand-coloured daisies survive just one splendid week out of the year. The clash between the warm currents running down from the Equator and the chilly streams rushing up from the South Pole sets things up so that at Cape Town, one may be able to enjoy a cheerful swim off one beach and freeze one's toes off on another. The climate that this congress of factors creates is quite remarkable, with gentle vineyards that thrive alongside an absolutely unique plant association called *fynbos.* It doesn't seem like much when we first look at it: *fynbos* appears to be made up of little plants, all of them the same and about a hand's height. If we adjust our sense of scale, however, we shall soon see that *fynbos* attains three times the density of plant species that is found in the Amazonian rain forest: 8,504 species scattered over thirty-five thousand square miles. The jewel of the *fynbos* are the protea, a genus of shrubs with alternate rigid leaves, dense flower heads resembling cones, and a fruit that is a hairy nut, another symbol of South Africa. As the name suggests — think of *protean,* meaning changeable — the protea can assume a thousand different forms. You will find it at the point of the Cape of Good Hope, where the oceans come together. Cape Point is just as it was when Bartolomé Diaz first sighted it four hundred years ago. It is a harsh rocky place. "The highest point in the world," as the South Africans insist on repeating. It is lovely up here. Every so often, the winds of the Roaring Forties carry the voice of the ghostly Flying Dutchman, who comes to keep Diaz company, amidst the grey waves where he lost his ship. The first outsiders to set foot on South African soil were the Chinese, with gracious apologies to Diaz and the Portuguese. As early as 1320, Chu-ss-pen, a cartographer who lived during the Mongol Dynasty (Yuan), drew a map bearing the unmistakable outline of the south of Africa. During the century that followed, between 1405 and 1433, no fewer than seven expeditions arrived in South Africa, with sixty-two junks and bearing forty thousand men. For the Europeans of this period, this was still considered *Terra Incognita*, uncharted territory. The Chinese left little trace of their presence, however. If one looks at the earliest European maps of the area (I had the honour and pleasure of being the guest of Oscar Norwich in Johannesburg, where he has assembled the finest collection of African maps), one will quickly note that the coasts are drawn with some degree of accuracy and care, while the interior is simply depicted in "grapevine fashion," a network of rivers and mountain chains, with a shadow to evoke an eternal sunset for those imagined phantasmagoric peoples with a single eye in the middle of their forehead. For the sailors who first explored South Africa, it was preferable to deal with the ocean monsters about which they though they knew something, than those mysterious inland menaces. Cape Town confuses the senses of even "inland navigators" like myself. In this lovely city, one has the historic expectation that one will be gazing out over an endless sea stretching all the way to the South Pole. That is a mistake. I headed south and immediately got lost in the centre of the downtown area. I was saved by Cecil Rhodes, the real one this time. In the botanical gardens I happened upon a statue. With a sweeping gesture, this stone Cecil Rhodes was pointing in a direction that seemed completely mistaken to me. The legend on the pedestal said: "There is your hinterland." One should never disobey a great explorer, however, and so I followed his command. And it was thus that I discovered that Cape Town looks northwestward, more in the direction of Brazil than towards the Antarctic. South Africa is tricky.

The cities of South Africa are not all alike, as is so often the case with the metropolises of the world. Cape Town was once called the Tavern of the Seas. In some sense, amidst the beauty of the setting of Table Mountain, which stands behind the city, offering it shelter, Cape Town has preserved this aspect of a place of passers-through, a classic seaport town. It was founded in 1652 by the Dutch navigator Jan van Riebeeck. His flagship was called the "Drommedaris," like the sand-dwelling "ship of the desert." Less than apt: van Riebeeck ignored the continental interior entirely. He settled down to gardening, raising vegetables and setting up vineyards. From the sailor's point of view, fresh fruit and vegetables are the remedy for scurvy, and alcoholic beverages cheer the spirit wonderfully during long sea voyages. Even now, Cape Town is a place where one feels cheerful, as one is inevitably at the end of one long voyage and at the beginning of another. This is a pleasant way station.

Johannesburg is entirely different. It is a city that has no history, only news accounts. When flying overhead, one sees immense mounds of shifted earth. The colour is yellowish and unhealthy-looking. These are the discarded wastes of the gold mines. If you set foot on the ground,

20 *The monument honouring Cecil John Rhodes, set at the entrance to the University of Cape Town. Rhodes became emblematic of the pioneer spirit exhibited during the second phase of South African history: specifically, we refer to the development of mining and the exploitation of mineral resources, as over against the farming practised by the earliest Dutch and Huguenot settlers, the so-called "Boers" (a word that means, quite simply, "peasant") Rhodes left Great Britain and went to South Africa in 1870, at the young age of seventeen, ridden with tuberculosis which he hoped to cure in this new land; his brother was farming cotton in Natal. The following year, the diamond rush of Griqualand exploded, and the two Rhodes brothers took part. In 1880, Rhodes had already formed the De Beers Company, still today the most powerful company in the world in the field of diamonds. His fortune grew even more, and by 1893 he had become the unquestioned boss of the mining industry (diamonds had now been joined by gold) as well as of farming in all of southern Africa. The only dream that he never managed to attain was that of founding a British Empire that would stretch without a break from the Cape of Good Hope to the Mediterranean, which he hoped to symbolize in a railroad running all the way from Cape Town to Cairo.*

you will hear distant rumbles and roars, and every so often a tiny earthquake: at Jo'burg — as the inhabitants refer to it — the digging and dynamiting goes on twenty-four hours a day. The downtown area is reminiscent of the straight-line arrangements of the camp of brawling miners which gave the city its birth. The city may stretch heavenward with its rows of skyscrapers, but deep beneath it are miles of shafts and galleries. The city is an improbable creation. It was originally a stretch of wind-swept arid savannah. The discovery of gold caused such a fever that those who wished to build a house here would often rove around nearby towns, stealing sheet metal. The city was growing so fast that there was a terrible shortage of materials for construction. After its poverty-stricken childhood and its turbulent adolescence, Johannesburg could hardly expect anything but a staid middle class adulthood. Observing its frenetic and chaotic development, one may fear the onset of senility. Aside from Cape Town and Johannesburg, South Africa has other major cities, such as Durban, which seems to hover between the two extremes, between history and adventure, between colourful past and hardboiled present. The urban appearance, actually and paradoxically, is given by the thousand overgrown villages that constitute the true heart of the country. Here people still live clustered around the bell tower of the local church and the little marketplace where one can buy anything imaginable: from headache tablets to saddles and rifles. This is a South Africa that may be slated for an early death: the modern world cannot afford anachronisms. When strolling on the lovely beaches of Durban, when walking through the New York-style department stores at Jo'burg, when inspecting the historic streets of Cape Town, when chatting with a scrubbed smiling grandmother at the front gate of a vineyard, with a little house in the background, one naturally asks oneself: "Where is Africa?"

But there is not one Africa that is "more authentic" than another. Baobabs and petunias, miners and nomads armed with spears, airplanes and rude carts, cattle and lions — all this is Africa. In particular, like everyone else, I love the savannah: a limitless plain, with thorny acacia trees, and spectacular sunsets... and the leopards, elephants, giraffes, antelopes, lions, and apes. There is little we can do about it — a glimpse of the savannah takes us back to the lives of our ancestors. And this is Africa, mother of us all. In the natural parks of South Africa and in the reserves that surround those parks, anything at all can happen: I once followed a leopard for two full hours, only to discover that it had been hunting and had finally caught a mouse; I was once approached by a rhinoceros that wished to find out why I was poking through its stool (I begin to wonder myself); I have seen lionesses hunting by night, and I have heard their asthmatic rasping cough (forget about roaring, that is the sound of an attacking lion) directly behind the little hut in which I lay sleeping.

21 top *The little town of Paarl and the valley of the Berg River serve here as a backdrop to the monument built in 1975 to commemorate the formation of the Afrikaans language. Based on Old Dutch, which was spoken by the first settlers, Afrikaans then incorporated an overlay of French from the Huguenot settlers, as well as a percentage of the autochthonous languages of Khoisan, spoken by Bushmen and Hottentots, the Bantu languages of black settlers from the north, Malaysian and Indonesian, and — lastly — English. In this monument, designed by Jan van Wijk, the three linked columns represent the European contributions, the three round shapes represent the African contributions, and the wall symbolizes the Malaysian contribution. A fountain symbolizes new ideas, and a stele that towers one hundred and eighty-seven feet in height, represents the growth of the Afrikaans language.*

21 bottom *The Council Hall, or Raadzaal, of Bloemfontein, the capital of the Orange Free State, stronghold of the white minority of Dutch descent, the Boers, was built in 1893 to replace the smaller and older raadzaal that had been in use since 1854 and which can still be seen in Saint George Street. Bloemfontein takes its name from a spring, near which Johannes Brits established the first settlement in 1840. The spring was known to the original inhabitants as the Manguang, meaning "the place of the leopard," but the Europeans chose to call it the "Fountain of Flowers," because of the luxuriant flora found throughout the area. Before a permanent settlement was set up here, Bloemfontein had been a stopover for the Voortrekkers, the Dutch farmers who were seeking independence from English rule.*

Amidst the sands of the Kalahari desert, I have helped porcupines caught in the dunes and I have greeted a newly rescued family of owls that a friend presented to me. In the dense woodlands of the Kruger National Park I have tracked jackals and have spent hours with my gaze locked onto the movements of a group of giraffes. In the meanwhile, all sorts of birds passed unobserved overhead. On the brutally harsh coasts of Tsitsikamma, while the Polar Ocean was gathering itself for the next wave, uncovering the rocks, I searched for elephants lost amidst the trees of the forest primeval. And now, like ghosts of an Africa that may no longer exist tomorrow, the white lions of Timbavati appear before my eyes.

South Africa is a modern nation and nature is a philosophical concept: all the world has been taken over by humans. This means that the wonders of fur, feathers, scales, and all under the African sun will require a particularly stringent management if they are to survive. Specialized computers and ecologists, selective hunting in order to control populations, planned fire-setting, forced migrations, are all part of a coherent and spectacular management of nature. To those who remember (or think they remember) a freer and wilder Africa, it is worth pointing out that this is the only way to ensure that the savannah animals of our dreams will prosper, and indeed survive.

The surface area of South Africa is close to half a million square miles, and on it live close to forty million inhabitants. Among its natural beauty, impressive landscapes, wild animals, diamonds and gold, these humans are what give South Africa its personality. Once again, let us relegate to the background the cities, where cultural and genetic homogenization have created masses of very similar individuals, involved in the sorts of activities that people engage in in all of the cities on earth. It is in the microcosms of villages scattered throughout the huge trackless landscapes that we will find the diversity of the South African population, which is structured on a genetic multiplicity (or racial, as the objectionable term once was), interwoven with a history that dates back to the dawn of human life on earth.

I remember a little song that was quite popular in South Africa a number of years ago. It was called "The Hat," and it went cheerfully like this, with a booming staccato of hidden information: "What is your name? / Who are your parents? / Where do you come from? / What is your tribe? / At what spring do you drink? / Take off your hat. We have lost our land." Anthropologically speaking, the "tribal" peoples (if we accept this definition) no longer exist in South Africa, following the contact with European "civilization," which has so altered the concept of cultural identity among the various ethnic groups, and which has changed the work they do and the lives they lead. A miner from Johannesburg, whether he speaks Sotho, Xhosa, or Zulu,

22 *A free climber dares the sheer cliffs along the waterfall of the Eland River in the eastern Transvaal. The waterfall is seven hundred and fifty feet high, and from the highlands drops away toward the low-lying lands of the savannah that lead to the Kruger National Park. The vertical distance between the two climatic zones can be more than thirty-three hundred feet: from luxuriant mountain vegetation to the aridity of the savannah below.*

has very little in common with the social and economic ways of life that were the foundation of the lives led by his ancestors a couple of centuries ago, and even more recently than that. And yet, if we wander across the land, South Africa still offers glimpses of ancient cultures.

One can begin with the hills of Zulu territory in Natal. This land is as shapely as the Zulu women (or, if you like, as fat as the Zulu men). Even the *idlu*, or traditional dome-roofed huts, seem like breasts jutting out from the earth. This is a land of strolls along the roads of red earth that run from village to scattered village. Here, if you meet a woman and you want to know who she is, where she comes from, how she feels, or what she is thinking about, do not look in her eyes — peek at her beads. The Zulus, like every African people, are wild about beads and colourful jewellery that contrasts in some way with the monochromatic landscape that surrounds them.

The Zulus make a veritable language of beads. A woman in love might send an *incwadi*, or a letter in beads. White stands for love, black is grief and loneliness, pink indicates poverty and green stands for jealousy; yellow is the wealth of gold while dark blue is loyalty. A set of colours, after the red of desires (it is odd how colours give shared sensations to all humans) is the seed of doubt.

The problem in South Africa has been that for many years these poetic languages were understood only within closed tribal groups. The signals of the Tswana were not understood by the Bhaca, even though their languages are very close. Zulu and Xhosa, the great adversaries of modern South Africa, both form part of the Bantu group of the Nguni: they were separated by a fierce war of conquest carried on by the Zulus less than two centuries ago. And even the Boers, of Dutch descent, look askance upon the trading and business aristocracy of the English, whom they consider late-comers and interlopers.

The reunification of the tribes — be they black, white, or Asian — is a complicated process, and constitutes the new social frontier of South Africa. It will be necessary to study more closely the history of each group, abandoning old and ridiculous claims. Archaeology shows that the areas and Johannesburg and Pretoria were once home to a Tswana people (shepherds, farmers, and miners), five hundred years before a Dutchman set foot at Cape Town. Therefore it is a false myth that claims that South Africa was settled by blacks and whites at the same time.

The only people that should be concerned about this information are now dead: today, the Khoisan (Hottentots and Bushmen) are gone. And yet it was they who were the lords of the green meadows of the Cape, or the lush and abundant hunting grounds of the valleys at the foot of the Drakensberg mountains. These peoples were isolated for such a great extent of time that they took on physical and linguistic characteristics that are unique in the world. The Khoisan were practically yellow in colour, they had a sort of false Mongolian fold to their eyes, and

23 *Oudtshoorn is the most important town of the Little Karoo, to the north of George, in the Cape province. It still represents the most important centre for ostrich ranching. Nowadays, the main product of this animal is the meat, but before the First World War, ostrich feathers from this area were sold at a price that was higher, ounce for ounce, than the price of gold. Around the town, one can still admire the extravagant mansions built by the "ostrich-plume barons," who were ruined when the society women of Europe stopped wearing feathers in their hats.*
At the height of production, the ostrich ranchers of Oudtshoorn were raising 750,000 ostriches, with annual exports of nearly half-a-million kilograms, or five hundred and the fifty short tons, of ostrich plumes every year. Nowadays, on the ranches, it is possible to ride the ostriches, which are raced at special ostrich-tracks.

24-25 *A family of elephants at a watering hole in the Addo National Park. This protected area, quite small in size (eighty-six hundred hectares, or 21,250 acres), lies about forty-five miles to the north of Port Elizabeth. There is a concentration of elephants three times that found anywhere else in Africa. The most famous elephant here is a female known as Afslurpie ("short trunk"). This matriarch (among elephants, the females lead the herd, and the only males in a herd are the pups) managed to survive the loss of the tip of her trunk in an accident. The trunk is an exceedingly sensitive organ that is crucial to a pachyderm's survival: it is used to smell, to drink, to feed, to explore the surrounding environment, and to protect the young.*

they spoke in clicking sounds. The most ancient forms of pictorial art known on earth were the work of the little Bushmen who lived in a cavern on the border with Namibia, a cave that now bears the surrealistic name of Apollo 11. Here, twenty-five thousand years ago, for the first time, a man painted on a rock a depiction of an animal. The Bushmen have left all over South Africa an immense picture gallery in the open air, in which — amidst images of an astounding naturalism and beauty — we can read the metaphors of a people swept away by history in the course of a couple of centuries. I remember once, after having wandered at length through the caves and rock-shelters of the Drakensberg, on foot and by horse, Paul Miles and I returned to the base (Miles is the curator of the rock paintings). After having spent days in a courteous and lovely universe full of antelopes, dances, hunting, animal-men, and human-creatures, amidst natural colours and earth-tones, we thought of a mutual friend who had once told us how his grandfather had taken part in the attack on the last surviving family of Bushmen.

"They were stealing cattle," was the explanation. "When we found him, riddled with bullets," continued the story, "the man no longer had any flesh on his thumb, from all the arrows he had been shooting at us. But his family had disappeared." Paul and I continued to hope that the family had somehow survived, for another fifty years, in the paintings. We stopped talking that evening, and drank ourselves senseless.

Wandering through South Africa, I have met a Zulu truck driver who wanted to become an anthropologist in order to avoid the painful initiation rites of his people; I have drunk the curdled milk of the Tswana shepherds; in an eighteen-hour journey by truck I have crossed the Kalahari desert to play in a rugby match with a team of Afrikaaners who nearly slaughtered me with the ball, and then plied me with an enormous quantity of beer and took me home over another eighteen hours of desert driving. I have chased after the graceful rump of a small leopard that was going to have breakfast on its favourite acacia tree. I have eaten Malaysian food at Cape Town and pigs' ears Portuguese-style in Johannesburg. I have toured the mine shafts and have tried to dance with the Bhaca (the colour of miners, come to think of it, is black no matter where you go) - the dance of the rubber boots. I have carried a tray of unpolished diamonds in Kimberley. I have attempted to lift a gold ingot in Jo'burg because they told me that if I succeeded, I could keep the ingot. I have walked a great deal and I have just not seen enough. Today, the "separate world" of South Africa can open without reservations, without sanctions, without isolation. We should all be witnesses to a great leap forward for Southern Africa and for the rest of the continent. Let Mandela, De Klerk, Buthelezi, and all of the people of South Africa accept our wishes of good fortune.

Water, Rocks, and Sunshine

26 top From high up on the Garden Route, one of the most scenic highways in the entire Cape province, between Mossel Bay and the mouth of the Storms Rivers, one can admire the dark blue expanse of the Indian Ocean. Here the seascape comes into contact with rocky extrusions profoundly carved by rivers and mountain streams. Many areas of the zone are protected: here, in fact, can be found the last stretches of primeval forests found in southern Africa, in particular in the enchanting park of Tsitsikamma.

26 bottom This photo depicts the remarkable alpine vegetation of the Drakensberg mountains, in the Royal Natal National Park, especially the so-called "cabbage tree" (Cussonia paniculata). The Zulus that live in this area thoroughly grind its roots and use the resulting substance to treat malaria. The park lies in the northernmost extremity of Natal, in the centre of a remarkable natural amphitheatre, beneath the towering Mont-aux-Sources and Lesotho.

27 The light of sunset colours the erosion-created arches of the Wolfberg (the "Mountain of the Wolf"), in the Cedarberg chain, Namaqualand, Cape Province. These sandstone mountains have been subjected over the millennia to the erosive actions of wind and water, and here one can find spectacular pinnacles shaped like a Maltese cross, caverns and canyons, peaks and tablelands, and even such savage pieces of architecture as the arches shown here.

28-29 From this escarpment in the park of the same name, one can look out over the Great Karoo. These crags are home to Verreaux's eagle (Aquila verreauxi), nearly thirty-nine inches in length, with a wingspan of about five feet; it lives chiefly on rock dassies, or hyraxes (Procavia capensis), which are small animals similar to a marmot, but actually close relatives of the elephant. The park of Karoo, not far from Beaufort West, is particularly interesting in that its rocks contain large amounts of dinosaur fossils dating from a period ranging from 250 to 150 million years ago, when the area was a vast swamp.

30-31 The Valley of the Thousand Hills lies between Pietermaritzburg and Durban, in the province of Natal. This spectacular formation is crossed by the river Mgeni (its name means "the Place of Acacias") and is inhabited by the Debe peoples. During the wars with the Zulu invaders, the Debe were driven to practise canibalism: this fact has given this valley a grim reputation, so that many areas here are abandoned and uninhabited. The temperatures in summer are very high.

The edge of the mountain

32-33 The rocky peaks that tower above the gorge of the river Blyde, in the eastern Transvaal, are known as the Three Huts. At the edge of the gorge, which is 2,624 feet deep from the bottom to the peak of the scarp, is the Overvaal Blydepoort Resort, with chalets and camp grounds, the base camp for hikers and horseback riders setting out along this "edge of the mountain," as the South Africans call it.

33 top The Great Karoo, at the centre of Cape Province, is an arid place, in which only the plants that need very little water flourish, such as this Aloe dichotoma, known also as the "quiver tree." Even today, its hollowed stems are used by the Bushmen, who are hunter-gatherers, for quivers for their poisoned arrows. Between June and July, this tall, much-branched tree produces spectacular blooms that attract birds, insects, and baboons; the big apes are so fond of the sweet pollen that they will destroy every flower on the tree before it can mature.

33 bottom Despite the partially arid appearance, a few drops of rain in the Great Karoo is quite enough to trigger the hundreds of species of small bushes — the main type of plantlife here — to flower in the most spectacular of fashions. The livestock ranchers (chief resource in the Karoo) are thoroughly familiar with the life-cycles of these little bushes, which provide the land with a uniform cover; were they not present, the sun would scald and crack the soil. By rotating the grazing of the livestock in accordance with the various seasons of flowering, the ranchers are capable of grazing large flocks of sheep on a territory that would appear to be lifeless.

34-35 The Blyde River runs through the eastern Transvaal. The name of the river means "joy," in memory of the meeting between a group of women certain that their husbands were dead and a number of Voortrekkers (Boers seeking independence from the English) led by Hendrik Potgieter in 1840. Before plunging into a spectacular gorge, the river carved in the sandstone odd shapes, known as the "pits of Bourke," after a gold prospector who enjoyed some success uphill from here.

36 The Lisbona Falls, just four miles from Graskop, are in the eastern Transvaal. This spectacular view is part of the Panorama Route, a highway that runs around a circular route about forty-five miles in length, running from Graskop, and passing through the gorge of the Blyde River, to the gold-laced rocks of Pilgrim's Rest, and then winds back to Graskop. This is the best route for getting to know the "edge of the mountain," as the escarpment is called here that separates the Drakensberg highlands from the plains that run down to Mozambique.

37 *This picture shows the distinctive vegetation of the Transvaal, in the mountainous areas that form the eastern border of this region. The predominant plants are the aloes and the tree ferns (the most common one being* Cythea dregei), *plants that are capable of withstanding the erratic levels of rainfall and the violent leaps in temperature that occur in these mountains, both on a daily-nightly basis and over the course of the year.*

38-39 *The Blyde River, in the eastern Transvaal, seen from the base of the escarpment that rises to an elevation of more than sixty-five hundred feet. From this point, the Blyde rolls on to join the river Olifants which, in turn, flows into the Limpopo.*

Castles in
the air

40-41 *This alpine meadow has as a backdrop the chain of the Drakensberg Mountains, in the province of Natal. Here we are not far from Injasuti, in the Giant's Castle Game Reserve. Before the arrival of white and black settlers, this had been the hunting grounds of the Bushmen, the earliest San inhabitants of South Africa. At that time, instead of cattle, immense herds of land antelopes grazed here, the symbols of spiritual power and of rain to the Bushmen, who were hunters and*

gatherers. The rock-shelters found in these mountains are dotted with spectacular rock-paintings, symbolic of the shamanistic voyages through the lands of the spirit, voyages that took place during a trance-like state. At Injasuti, on a sandstone wall, one can still admire the depiction of a battle between Good and Evil.

41 *The amphitheatre of Mont-aux-Sources, in the Drakensberg Mountains in Natal, is the source of the Tugela River. The most important river in Natal tumbles forth atop a peak at an altitude of 10,765 feet. Then it plunges down some sixty-five hundred feet, through a series of waterfalls and rapids that are the highest and most spectacular in South Africa. The amphitheatre is closed off to the east by a tableland known as the Eastern Buttress, upon which one can see the Devil's Peak, one of the most difficult and dangerous peaks to climb in this region.*

42-43 *The Mostertshoek Twins, in Cape Province, are of course twin peaks. Rising to an elevation of 6,662 feet, they mark the beginning of a pass which was opened in 1760 by Jan Mostert, who was following the course of the river Breë. In 1846, under the command of Andrew Bain, four hundred convicts sentenced to hard labour built the first road through the pass, which was thereafter named Michell's Pass, in honour of a high official of the Cape Province. For thirty years, this pass was the only route to the north of the country.*

44-45 *The Hottentots-Holland Mountains are the backdrop in this photograph of a stallion farm of the Broadlands ranch. This is not far from Stellenbosch, one of the best known regions of vineyards and vintners in all of South Africa. The mountains keep in the humidity from the Atlantic Ocean, creating a microclimate of the Mediterranean variety.*

46-47 In late August, along the strip of coastline to the north of Cape Town, in Namaqualand, there are magnificent spontaneous blooms that create landscapes so spectacular as to take one's breath away. With its 4.75 inches of rain every year, Namaqualand is one of the most arid regions in all of South Africa. And yet these rains, typical of a true desert, are sufficient to trigger the blooming of millions of flowers, especially daisies of every hue imaginable, although they live only for a few days. The colours are arranged in a uniform manner, as if they had been organized by a gardener, because each of the species has specific territories in which they flourish.

48-49 *From this beach along the Garden Route, in the Cape Province, one looks out over the Indian Ocean, directly toward Antarctica: there is no land between the hot sands and the continent of ice. On the horizon is the route of the Roaring Forties, a path followed particularly by captains of sailing vessels. At this latitude the fierce winds will drive a ship around the world without once making land.*

50 *False Bay is the broad gulf that opens out to the east of the peninsula of the Cape, closing off to the south the area of Cape Town proper. The name is derived from the fact that the ships that arrived from the east often mistook Cape Hangklip for the Cape of Good Hope. Certain that they were now in the Atlantic Ocean, these ships often had considerable difficulties in getting free of the powerful currents that formed at the mouth of the bay. The sands that are accumulated by the drift of the currents inside the bay, near Cape Hangklip, have a remarkable silvery hue.*

51 *The bay of Chapman, on the western side of the Cape Peninsula, has chilly and treacherous waters. It is a surfer's paradise on earth, however, and has some of the largest and fastest waves in all of South Africa. The bay takes its name from a certain John Chapman, a sailor who landed in 1607 from the British ship Consent to seek a good location for mooring, but who was abandoned on these shores. The place where Chapman managed to survive has the oldest English place-name in the history of South Africa.*

52 *The entrance of the bay of Knysna, known as "the Head," can be seen from the Garden Route, in the Cape Province. The bottleneck that leads to the lagoon of this little town, which was once a major centre in the hardwood trade, has always created problems for the ships that attempt to enter here,* *beginning with the brigantine* Emu, *that sank like a shot here in 1817. More than two hundred species of fish live in this lagoon, which is also renowned for its oysters. Inland, behind Knysna, there are still patches of the primeval forest, whose hardwoods made the place's fortune.*

53 top *South African beaches are often wedged between ocean and mountains. This makes them particularly lovely, and allows for interesting hikes inland.*

53 bottom *This picture offers a fine view of the beach of Noetzie, which extends eastward from Knysna, where the river Noetzie (meaning "black") flows into a small lagoon. On the horizon, one can see the rocky point of Cape Seal, which separates this bay from the bay of Plattenberg.*

54-55 *Even though many of the beaches are exceedingly popular, the urban growth has always been moderated, the ocean is still clean, and the life forms found in the various environments are considered to be a valuable resource. Particularly interesting is the life of the reef, exposed at low tide.*

Urban Explorations

56 *The beach frontage of the city of Durban is a concentrate of wealth, luxury, and traditional style, characteristics which are reflected in the architecture of the hotels and homes.*

57 *Durban, which was founded as a haven for the much hounded ivory traders, who were always in danger from Zulu raids; nowadays it is a paradise of maritime attractions. Its beach frontage is known as the "Golden Mile" — this is where all of the luxury hotels and the main attractions of the city are concentrated.*

Durban, a mile of joy

58-59 *The Portuguese called Durban the "Rio de Natal"; they were the first, with the Portuguese navigator Vasco da Gama, to land there, on 25th December 1497. It was not until 1823 that Rio de Natal became the permanent residence of a group of traders led by Henry Fynn: their first settlement is where the old railroad station stood. In 1853 the city was renamed Durban, in honour of the governor of the Cape, Sir Benjamin d'Urban.*

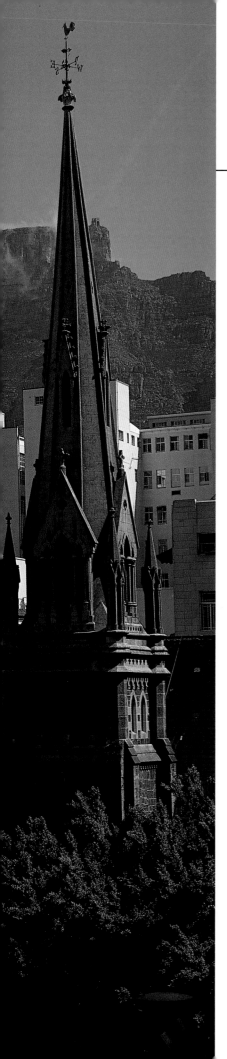

Cape Town, Tavern of the Seas

60-61 *Green Market Square is still at the heart of the traditions of Cape Town. It should not be forgotten that the city was founded specifically to provide mariners with supplies of fresh fruit and vegetables, after unbroken sea voyages of months. The architecture of the buildings that surround the fruit market, at the downtown corner of St. George Street, is still typical of the Cape, as well as featuring a number of distinctively Dutch buildings.*

61 top *Grand Parade, a large square that was originally the parade grounds, used for military drills, stands before the Castle of Good Hope. Although it has not lost its military character, and is used for official ceremonies, parades, and reviews, this square also hosts a number of markets, including a noted green market. The building in the background is the old City Hall, built in "Italian style" and completed in 1905. Today it is often used for concerts of classical music.*

61 bottom *The University of Cape Town is located at the base of Table Mountain, whose peaks rise to an elevation of thirty-three hundred feet; it is possible to take a cableway to the top.*

62-63 *Clifton is a residential suburb of Cape Town located at the base of the rocky formation known as the "Lion's Head," a granite peak that rises to the northwest of Table Mountain, in the background. Although the coastline is quite harsh, and the beaches are narrow and can only be reached by stone stairways, Clifton is an excellent place to sun and surf, though the water is quite chilly.*

64-65 *This picture shows an aerial view of Cape Town, with the harbour in the foreground and Table Mountain in the distance, looking south. Cape Town is the mother city of all South Africa. It was in fact in the bay of Cape Town that, in 1652, the Dutch captain Jan van Riebeeck moored his ship* Drommedaris. *The city, which was originally a fort and a series of orchards and gardens, was simply a way station on the route to the Indies. Its location, however, along with its safe harbour, made it with the passage of time into a sort of "Tavern of the Seas" for all the ship crews who were about to face, or had just overcome, the thousands of perils and threats of doubling the Cape of Good Hope. Even now, despite its modern buildings, Cape Town still has the distinctive atmosphere of a harbour city, where people and merchandise from all over the globe come together.*

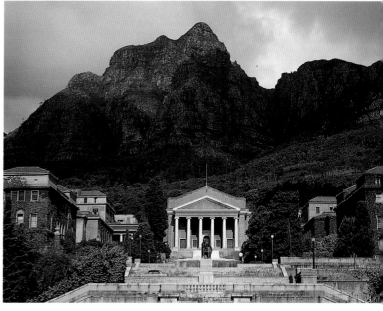

Johannesburg, the Eldorado of Africa

66 top   *The J.G. Strijdom Tower has become an integral part of the skyline of Johannesburg, as if it were a sort of giant lightning rod designed against the violent thunderstorms that are typical of the Transvaal. In reality, it is a communications tower that stands 882 feet high.*

66 bottom   *The Southern Sun Hotel in Johannesburg stands in the middle of the city. Here, there are very few buildings any older than thirty years; this is due to the incessant flow of wealth generated by the mining of gold, and to a constant growth in population that is unusual for South Africa. Nowadays, in the middle of Johannesburg, modern architecture triumphs, but the inhabitants still love to remember the sheet-metal roofs of the shacks that were there at the city's foundation.*

67   *In this aerial view we see Johannesburg, "the city that gold built." The arrangement into quadrants that distinguishes the centre of Johannesburg came from the original mining camps that grew feverishly as new veins of gold were found in the Rand, the richest hill on earth, just three miles from the centre of town. Beginning in 1886, when a certain George Harrison discovered the first veins of gold, Johannesburg has become richer and richer with the passage of time. The city was built from nothing at the precise orders of F.C. Eloff, an envoy of the president of the Transvaal, and it was named after two mining inspectors named Johannes.*

Pretoria,
the city of the Voortrekkers

68-69 *The purple flowers of the jacaranda* (Jacaranda mimosifolia) *are typical of the landscape of the Transvaal between Johannesburg and Pretoria. The tree, which belongs to the family* Bignoniaceae, *and comes from Brazil, has adapted perfectly to the climate of the South African highlands. The flowers bloom between October and November, after all the leaves have fallen.*

70-71 *The area surrounding modern-day Pretoria, the administrative capital of the Republic of South Africa, was settled in 1837 by a group of Voortrekkers. The leader of these frontiersmen was Andries Pretorius, who built his home in the middle of a large farm, the Grootplats, that lay at the confluence of the rivers Apies and Crocodile. With his*

brother, M.W. Pretorius, he became a fully-fledged hero of his people, due to the outstanding courage they displayed at the battle of Blood River. After his death, the Apies river valley was chosen by the Boers as the site of the new capital of the Republic of South Africa; the city was founded in November of 1855 and was named Pretoria, in honour of the Pretorius brothers.

Jacaranda City and other flowers

72 At the entrance of the Provincial Council Building of Pietermaritzburg stands a statue of Queen Victoria. The little town became the capital of Natal in 1843, and was home to a sizable garrison of British troops, ready for emergency raids to control the Zulu from close at hand. The city had a sort of pre-foundation, earlier, in 1838, by a group of Voortrekkers who had taken refuge in this area following a brutal fight with the Zulus. From the names of two captains of the badly beaten party — Piet Retief and Gert Maritz — the city took its name.

73 The architecture of the library of Port Elizabeth is a reminder of the city's earliest origins. Founded in 1799, overlooking Algoa Bay, following the construction of Fort Frederick by a garrison of British troops, Port Elizabeth takes its name from the wife of Sir Rufane Donkin, the deputy governor of the Cape, who established his residence here in 1820. Today, the city is the third-largest port of South Africa in terms of volume of trade, and the fifth-largest city in South Africa by population.

The lace of Flanders

74-75 *The architecture of the valleys that surround Cape Town is Dutch in style and origin. These areas of vineyards are quite prosperous, and have been ever since the earliest days of the settlement in the Cape: the production of wine from dried grapes was conducted in order to supply passing ships had in fact been one of the objectives of establishing the colony. In this area, the Dutch style has somehow been bolstered by decorative features with a distinctly baroque air to*

them, as one can clearly see in the gardens of Ormarins Manor (right), the church of Worcester (bottom left), the largest village in the valley of the Brëe, and in the entrance to the Dutch Reformed Church of Swellendam (top left) which, though it was built in 1910, still preserves intact the style of the church built on the same site in long-ago 1802. After Cape Town and Stellenbosch, Swellendam was the third settlement to be established by the Dutch West Indies Company, owned by van Riebeeck. By looking at the houses of these areas, one can sense the degree to which South Africans of Cape Town are still attached to venerable traditions.

Sun City, a Southern dreamscape

76-77 Located in Bophuthatswana, a former homeland that had been granted independence in 1977, Sun City is the South African equivalent of Las Vegas. It is a huge amusement park, with gambling as the most exciting attraction. Its location in an independent state (even though it is an enclave, entirely situated within South African territory) was a concession of the puritanical attitudes of South African legislators, who have long insisted on outlawing gambling, but the new constitution annexed the small independent enclave states, resulting in a radical change in the standing of Sun City. The city, which is located near Pilanesberg, occupies a mountainous amphitheatre in which one watches the highest-density rhinoceros population in Africa; it was founded in 1980, and it was planned and built in just one year by Sol Kerzner. The original core of the resort has grown at a dizzying rate: the lavish buildings of The Cascades (left) have been joined by the complex of the "Lost City" in 1992 — a luxurious tableau depicting a local legend.

A Mosaic of Peoples

78 top *Three women of the Ndebele group sit before a typical home outside of Pretoria. The Ndebele (whom Europenas call Matabele) belong, like the Zulus, to the Nguni group. Their name comes from a word in the Sotho language (the Sotho offered shelter to the fleeing Ndebele) that means "refugees." The Ndebele women have developed a complex code for decorating body and clothing with beads. In the Ndebele groups that have remained isolated nearby Pretoria, the same style of decoration has been transferred to the walls of the houses.*

78 bottom *Wind surfing can be considered as a metaphor for South Africa: liberty, movement, ocean, sand, forest, environment.*

79 *South Africa is a multiracial nation. As a state, it certainly was born white: the autochthonous Khoisan peoples (Bushmen and Hottentots) were nomads, and did not recognize the idea of ownership of land. The black-skinned Bantu peoples were also nomadic, and followed their herds of cattle as they grazed, and the variations of the weather. For white men who came here, South Africa was often their last chance. It is an irony of history that apartheid should have been created by a white minority that had often been subjected to political and religious persecution and discrimination in Europe, and that had finally found freedom on this distant shore of Africa.*

80-81 *In anthropological terms, there are no races: the smile of a girl whose features are so clearly Dutch as to identify her as a native of the Orange Free State, the land of the Boers, and the smile of a young Tsonga girl, whose parents are skilled Bantu fishermen in Natal, are both ways of expressing sweetness and serenity typical of* Homo sapiens, *the species to which we all belong.*

82 *The wedding shown in this photograph took place in Pietermaritzburg. The cultural assimilation of such European features as the wedding dress, is a price that has been paid by all of the peoples that were subjected to the burdens of colonialism. At the same time, this photograph hints at the development in South Africa of a black middle class, a crucial element needed for the political transition that is sweeping this country. The problem is to work things so that the true cultures, white and black, artificially kept separate for so long, should finally begin to mingle and grow in interdependence.*

83 *This photograph shows the congregation of Ladybrand, in the Orange Free State. This small town of shopkeepers and farmers not far from Lesotho still works as it did a century ago: on Sundays, the entire community goes to church to pray.*

The Dutch Reformed Church was one of the unifying elements that kept the Boers together over the years. And it is no accident that a number of areas of the Orange Free State are bitterly opposed to free votes, and are threatening to secede.

The white tribe

84-85 *Flowers and greenery can be found even inside the luxurious buildings that follow the European architectural tradition.*

86-87 and 87 top *England certainly deserves credit for the survival of the athletic tradition in South Africa. For the Boers, sports and entertainment were in some sense sinful. For an Englishman, sport is a way of life. And so, it is still possible, on Satudays, to witness a match of bowls in an elite like that of Bloemfontein (left) or cheer on a cricket match (top right). In contrast with what has long been believed by many, South African sports were never entirely segregated. It was more a matter of cultural and class distinctions that marked the various "tribes" in the different types of sports.*

87 bottom *The starting gate at the racetrack of Clairwood Park at Durban, in Natal, is shown just after the race begins. It is here that the July Handicap is held, the most important event in African horse racing. Around here, people still use horses to get from place to place and for work, so it should come as no surprise that the horse racing fever is still so strong.*

88-89 *On the coasts of Natal, waves break of every size and at every speed. The water temperature, milder than on the beaches of the Cape, the accommodation and other facilities, and its relative isolation make it a surfer's paradise.*

90-91 *The square of the Grand Parade, at Cape Town, spreads out before the old City Hall. The Coon Carnival marks the celebration of the new year. Of course, since South Africa lies to the south of the equator, it all takes place under a clear blue sky in mid-summer heat.*

At the end of the rainbow

92 top left *In this picture, one has a good view of the casting of an ingot of gold by the sort of technology that was used at the turn of the century. Not far from Johannesburg, a mining town has been rebuilt as it was, and it is possible to observe the techniques for mining and smelting gold. At the end of this demonstration, the ingot is set on a bench. Anyone who can lift it with one hand can keep it. So far, because of the slipperiness of gold and shape and weight of the ingot, no one has yet succeeded. But everyone tries.*

92 bottom left *A Tsonga (or Shangaan) of Natal gathers worms from the Mopane trees* (Colophospermum mopane). *The worms are actually the larva of a greyish-brown butterfly, the* Gonimbrasia belina, *and are dried for long conservation, or are eaten fried or roasted.*

92 right *The "white tribe" of South Africa is not made up only of the well-to-do. Some of the more humble jobs, such as processing precious stones, are done by white labourers.*

93 *A herd of ostriches runs in a compact group on a ranch on the Little Karoo. These animals are raised for their meat, the lowest in cholesterol of all meats eaten by humans.*

94-95 *The amphitheatre of the Mont-aux-Sources, in the Royal Natal National Park, rises behind one of the fifteen bungalows of the Tendele Camp. The accommodation in South African parks is always excellent and affordable, and must be reserved months in advance.*

Black is beautiful

96 top *The domed houses of the Zulus are called* indlu, *and are chiefly built of a framework of branches that supports interwoven reed mats. The traditional model, made entirely of plant material, is nowadays modified with elements made of unbaked earth, and in* tukul *shapes, typical of non-nomadic African homes. Nowadays, in fact, the Zulus are no longer nomadic shepherds, and their stable, sedentary life-style is reflected in their homes.*

96 bottom *A Zulu elder prepares a wooden club, or* kudokerrie, *which is used in hunting small animals. The Zulus are famed for their warrior spirit, and the* assagai — *the throwing spear of South African tribes, little more than a broad, short dagger with a haft — became a fearsome assault weapon for the conquests of the Ngnuni clan of Shaka, known as Zulu ("those of the heavens") beginning in 1816. With an assagai in hand, a Zulu warrior could neither fight from a distance nor retreat: nothing remained but certain death or victory.*

97 *This photograph presents the composed serenity of an apprentice fortune-teller of the Zulu people. The role of soothsayers (rather than "witch-doctors") remains that of interpreting the signs that are believed to be sent by the departed ancestors to the living. An apprentice must live with the master for many years, before being declared* isangoma. *The distinctive signs of a soothsayer are the swollen bladders of animals killed as sacrifices (bound up in the hair) and two little strips of leather, which belong to the first and to the last animal sacrificed during the period of learning fortune-telling techniques. The Zulus once distinguished between practitioners of white magic (*inyanga, *still common everywhere among herbalists and folk healers) and practitioners of black magic, the* isanusi, *capable of provoking or curing illnesses, at times even fatal illnesses. Today, the* isanusi *remain in hiding, and people generally turn to the* isangoma, *or simple fortune-tellers.*

98 The San (or Bushmen) were the first humans to inhabit South Africa. They have left rock paintings and carvings everywhere in the land, some dating back twenty-five thousand years. Their origins are still the subject of some debate, but it would appear that their somatic features (eyes with a false Mongolian fold, yellowish complexion, steatopygia, shortness) are the result of extended genetic isolation. Since they were hunter-gatherers, they quickly entered into conflict with the European colonists and the Bantu herders: both began campaigns of extermination, since the Bushmen could not distinguish between cows and sheep, on the one hand, and antelopes, on the other, which they had hunted freely for centuries. Today, in South Africa, the San are virtually extinct, while their cousins the Khoi-khoi (Hottentots) have been genetically assimilated into the larger mixed group referred to as "Coloured," which includes most of the inhabitants.

99 left *Beginning in 1991, among the Kagga Kamma, mountains of the Cedarberg in the Cape province, a questionable experiment has been underway, an attempt to return a group of San taken from the Kalahari to their life of hunting and gathering. Unfortunately, the San of Kagga Kamma cannot be self-sufficient, and they are forced to "perform" their way of life for tourists.*

99 right *An Ndebele woman poses in front of her remarkably decorated house not far from Pretoria. All of the Nguni peoples of South Africa show a marked love of colourful decoration done with beads. The phenomenon is typical of herding tribes, and seems to be prompted by the sensory deprivation that can result from long periods spent on the savannah, an exceedingly monochromatic landscape. The Nguni (and especially the Zulus) have actually developed a language of beads, according to which pink means poverty, red is tears, yellow is wealth, and green is jealousy. Depending on how a person arranges the beads, it is possible to express one's state of mind.*

100-101 *This picture shows two Shangaan women. The Shangaan are better known as the Tsonga, and they live along the border with Mozambique. Although they do not belong to the Nguni group, their costumes were influenced by the powerful rule of the Zulu, by whom they were subjugated. They had a mixed economy (agricultural and herding), but they differed from other peoples in the area because they are good fishermen, both in freshwater and in the ocean.*

A Noah's Ark

102 top *The young male Impala* (Aepyceros melampus) *is one of the most elegant types of antelope that can be observed in South Africa. It tends to live in areas that abound in dense bushes; it feeds on the leaves of the plants. It can weigh as much as one hundred and seventy-five pounds, and it is notorious* for the remarkable leaps — dozens of yards — which it executes with great agility. This type of ungulate began its evolutionary history here in South Africa when, two million years ago, all of the species in the area were subjected to great selective pressure because of a progressive encroachment of the deserts.

102 bottom *A colony of Cape Penguins* (Spheniscus demersus) *has settled on the island of Jutten, in the West Coast National Park, at the mouth of the bay of Saldanha, to the north of Cape Town. This species was once known as the Jackass Penguin, for its braying note, but it has since received a less insulting name. It is found along all of the southern and western coastlines of South Africa, but is declining in numbers because of pollution. The presence of these animals commonly found in Antarctica is encouraged by the icy currents (the most important one being the Benguela current) that sweep up from the South Pole.*

103 *In Kruger National Park, in the eastern Transvaal, it is quite common to encounter Elephants* (Loxodonta africana), *symbols at once of strength and weakness. Their size makes them immune to the predators of the savannah, but the ivory of the tusks has been the prize of the animal's near extinction, because of the intensive hunting done by that superpredator, the human being. The intelligent policies of the South African parks and the strict anti-poaching regulations have brought about a steady increase in the elephant population, so that in some cases it has been necessary to kill selected specimens, to ensure that the elephants do not outgrow their environment.*

104-105 *In Kruger National Park, in the eastern Transvaal, it is also quite common to encounter the Lion, the most admired animal in Africa. Often, however, the lion's behaviour is not quite up to its royal reputation. It often happens that a lioness* (right) *will fiercely reject the lion's advances; on the other hand, the lion does little to ensure it will have worthy heirs. All of the "work" of raising the young and hunting for food falls to the lionesses, which live in prides, together with a pair of male sires.*

106-107 *The Leopards* (Panthera pardus) *shown in this photograph live in the protected game reserve of Mala Mala, to the west of the Kruger National Park, in the eastern Transvaal. The Leopard on the right is probably a female, with a preadult specimen probably about to break free of the mother.*

108 *The vegetation of the Kruger National Park is that found typically in a wooded savannah. This is an environment marked by sharp shifts in seasons, with brief but violent rainstorms, and a long dry season. The lowlands of the Transvaal have always had a relatively humid climate, however, to the point that many border areas with Mozambique are often quite flooded. Here the climate is unhealthy, and malarial mosquitoes proliferate, so that the population over the centres has oscillated in conjunction with the rains and the consequential spread of the disease.*

109 left *The Aloe of the littoral species belonging to the family of the Liliaceae manages to survive even in conditions of extreme aridity, thanks to the supplies of water contained in the cells of its "succulent" leaves. The thorns serve only to reduce the evaporation of humidity found in the leaves, and also to protect them from herbivores. The latex that is exuded by the leaves when broken is exceedingly bitter: it has long been used in the manufacture of cosmetics, as long ago as during the rule of the pharaohs.*

109 right *A plant that is quite typical of the savannah is the so-called "fever tree"* (Acacia xanthophloea). *In Africa it was believed that this tree was in some way responsible for epidemics of yellow fever, perhaps because of the unhealthy colour of its bark. It is in any case true that this type of acacia, in comparison with its sister trees of the savannah, lives in wetter areas, where insects that carry life-threatening diseases proliferate.*

110-111 *In this picture one can admire the mother and pup of the White Rhinoceros* (Ceratotherium simum), *in Natal. In South Africa, and especially in the park of Natal, lives the greatest number of rhinoceroses in Africa. Unlike the Black Rhinoceros* (Diceros bicornis) *it is peaceful by nature, and lives only on grasses that it grazes. The shape of the neck and the weight of the head are such that it is almost unable to lift its eyes from the ground. A White Rhinoceros (the colour in its name comes from the fact that the first naturalists saw this animal covered in dust) can weigh nearly five tons.*

112 *The observation of wild animals in nature is one of South Africa's prime tourist attractions. Millions of visitors follow the tracks of the Kruger Natural Park each year. Private reserves have also been opened, which give more room to the animals, and attract much of the flow of tourists. In these reserves, in fact, one can follow the animals in open cars, which is forbidden in the parks: the excitement grows when one encounters big cats, such as a pride of Lions* (top) *or a Leopard* (bottom). *This is nature within reach.*

113 *Even though the hospitality structures inside the Kruger Park are first-rate, private reserves, such as Mala Mala or Sabie Sabie, offer greater opportunities to get close to the place. The accommodation for tourists is often old farmhouses in which the owners of the land once lived. The atmosphere takes us back to the nineteenth century, and one has the illusion that nothing in Africa has changed since then.*

114 and 115 top *Impalas live by eating leaves, and are therefore generally found in wooded environments. As is the case with the European stag the females have no horns* (left). *They gather into sizable harems, subject to only one male, whose horns appear to be used as attractive attributes* (top), *so as to lure females and to compete with other males in the creation of a harem. Antelopes are fundamental to the survival of the environment: they eat the fruit of plants found in the area, and spread the seeds in their faeces.*

115 centre *Burchell's Zebra* (Equus burchelli burchelli) *takes its name from the great naturalist, William Burchell, who led the first scientific expedition to South Africa, in 1811. In four years, he gathered eighty-seven hundred samples of plants and described many new animals. The South African zebra is distinct from the East African zebra in that, between one black stripe and the next, there is a narrower brown stripe.*

115 bottom *The Giraffe* (Giraffa camelopardalis) *is a familiar sight in the savannah landscape. Its improbably long neck, used in feeding on the acacia treetops, becomes a problem when the giraffe wishes to drink. The animal is then forced to spread its forelegs in a manner that makes it exceedingly vulnerable to predators.*

115

116-117 *The Blue, or Brindled, Wildebeest* (Connochaetes taurinus) *is called the clown of the savannah. One can encounter herds of millions, mingling with zebras. The males are solitary and territorial, while the females meet them on their own territory. Births are synchronized throughout the herd: the young are birthed over a period of a week to ten days. In this manner, the predators are able to kill only a few of them: even the belly of a lion has a limit.*
The onomatopoeic term "gnu" (another type of wildebeest) comes from the word used by the Khoi-khoi to imitate its cry.

117 *The Spotted Hyena* (Crocuta crocuta) *is quite willing to take advantage of the availability of the young of savannah-dwelling herbivores to enjoy some succulent meals. Unlike what is widely believed, this animal obtains food chiefly by hunting. It lives in matriarchal clans: it is one of the very cases in which a female mammal is generally larger than the male.*

118 top *At Saint Lucia, the best place for observing crocodiles* (Crocodylus niloticus), *is Cape Vidal, where there is a science centre devoted to this giant reptile, a throwback to prehistoric times. This species dates back three hundred million years, and it survived the extinction of the dinosaurs. If one observes carefully the rear paws of a crocodile, one may note that they appear to belong to a biped, and that they are longer than the forepaws (they also have one less digit). The crocodile is just a sort of tyrannosaurus that, in order to survive, went to live in the water.*

119 left *The Saddle-Billed Stork* (Ephippiorhynchus senegalensis), *or jabiru; this picture shows a male specimen, recognizable by the golden drop beneath its bill, on its neck; it was photographed in the lake of Saint Lucia, where it is an infrequent resident. It lives in shallow waters, where it feeds. It is five feet tall, with a wing-span close to nine feet.*

119 right *The Ground Hornbill* (Bucorvus leadbeateri) *is a common bird on the east coast of South Africa. It is about the size of a turkey. In this photograph, a male specimen is shown; females have a blue blotch on their gullets. Essentially earth-bound (hence the name), they live in flocks of four to ten individuals. They take flight only when disturbed or to take shelter in the trees in which they nest. Their song, which is a deep sound, is often heard around dawn. They prefer lowland or scrubland environments.*

118 bottom *A group of Hippopotamuses* (Hippopotamus amphibius) *lolls in the waters of the lagoon of Santa Lucia, in Natal. This area, practically on the border with Mozambique, is a paradise for naturalists. Here the freshwater flows of many rivers mingle with the warm currents of the Indian Ocean. The animals have adapted to the salty water: nonetheless it is suprising to see a fresh-water pachyderm such as the Hippopotamus just a few yards from the* ocean. *Among other things, the Hippopotamus has a very delicate skin: that is why it cannot remain long out of water. Often one notes that the skin exudes a reddish substance: many nineteenth-century observers recounted tales of Hippopotamuses that, when hunted, "sweated blood." In reality, it is a sort of protective cream. We do not know enough about these delicate regulatory mechanisms in a marine environment.*

120 *This male Ostrich* (Struthio camelus) *was photographed in the Kalahari Gemsbok National Park. The Ostrich is the largest living bird, and it is flightless. The females are brownish in colour, in order to blend in with their favourite habitat, the open and arid savannah. The male is black and white, since it is in charge of* brooding eggs at night. In the Kalahari, a semidesert, it is possible to see hundreds of Ostriches gathering around a pool of water; usually they live in herds of about forty individuals, except during the mating season. An Ostrich can attain speeds of 40 mph, and maintain those speeds for considerable distances.

121 *Beyond a region of red dunes, the Kalahari appears as an endless grassland plain. Here the climate is extreme: in July it may range from torrid temperatures during the day to a few degrees below zero during the night. Toward the end of August, clouds gather on the horizon, and spectacular rainstorms can occur. Despite the apparent desolation, the Kalahari is capable of supporting a rich array of fauna with numerous different food chains, ranging from caterpillars to Lions.*

122-123 *The vegetation found on the slopes of the dunes of the Kalahari is made up of a wide array of species of bushes and grasses that are particularly resistant to arid landscapes.*
The Mother Grass (Stipagrostis sp.), *for example, enlarges its stalks so as to create shade near the roots. This ensures sufficient humidity for the plant itself, as well as encouraging the growth of other plant and animal species in that cover.*

123 *The southern part of the Kalahari, on the border between Botswana and South Africa, receives greater precipitation because of its latitude and proximity to the Atlantic Ocean. The level of rainfall (less than eight inches annually) makes it a desert, but is sufficient to trigger a rapid and simultaneous flowering of all plants immediately after a cloudburst.*

124-125 *Among the desert dunes, there are strange creatures to be found in the Kalahari Gemsbok National Park. This beetle* (Psammodes sulcicollis) *is known here as the* toktokkie, *after the sound it produces by striking its chitinous abdomen against the sandy ground.*

126-127 *The Cape Sea Lion* (Arctophalus pusillus) *forms large colonies along the arid coasts of Namaqualand and of the desert of Namib, where it is encouraged to reside by the icy Antarctic currents. It can be distinguished from seals by the presence of auricles.*

128 *The cheetah* (Acinonyx jubatus) *is the fastest land mammal on earth: it can attain speeds of 75 mph. Because of its speed, it can catch gazelles on the open plain, where it particularly loves to hunt.*